LET'S PLAY

# Golf

**Aaron Carr**

# LET'S READ
## AV2 BY WEIGL™
### ADDED VALUE • AUDIO VISUAL

Go to **www.av2books.com**, and enter this book's unique code.

## BOOK CODE

**E330130**

**AV² by Weigl** brings you media enhanced books that support active learning.

AV² provides enriched content that supplements and complements this book. Weigl's AV² books strive to create inspired learning and engage young minds in a total learning experience.

# Your AV² Media Enhanced books come alive with...

**Audio**
Listen to sections of the book read aloud.

**Video**
Watch informative video clips.

**Embedded Weblinks**
Gain additional information for research.

**Try This!**
Complete activities and hands-on experiments.

**Key Words**
Study vocabulary, and complete a matching word activity.

**Quizzes**
Test your knowledge.

**Slide Show**
View images and captions, and prepare a presentation.

# ... and much, much more!

Published by AV² by Weigl
350 5th Avenue, 59th Floor
New York, NY 10118

Website: www.av2books.com        www.weigl.com

Library of Congress Control Number: 2013941104
ISBN 978-1-48961-762-0 (hardcover)
ISBN 978-1-48961-763-7 (softcover)

Printed in the United States of America in North Mankato, Minnesota
1 2 3 4 5 6 7 8 9 0  17 16 15 14 13

062013
WEP220513

Project Coordinator: Aaron Carr        Designer: Mandy Christiansen

Weigl acknowledges Getty Images, iStockphoto, and Alamy as the primary image suppliers for this book.

# LET'S PLAY

# Golf

## CONTENTS

I love golf.
I am going to play golf today.

# Tee Time

Kids tee off closer to the hole than adults.

I get dressed to play golf. I wear pants and a shirt with a collar.

# Dressing Up

Most golf courses have a strict dress code.

I have many golf clubs.
Each of my golf clubs
is different.

# Aiming High

**Higher numbered clubs hit the ball higher in the air.**

9

I go to the golf course to play. The course has 18 holes for me to play.

# On the Range

Some golf courses have a driving range.

I warm up
before starting to play.
I practice swinging my club
and putting the ball.

## Like a Pro

**Pro golfers practice every day.**

I meet my friends at the first hole. We hit our first shots off a tee.

Golfers take turns playing their shots.

15

I hit the golf ball into the hole. I try to take fewer shots than my friends.

# For the Win

The lowest score wins in golf.

Sometimes, I play on a team with my friend. We play against two other players.

Teammates take turns hitting the same ball.

I love golf.

# GOLF FACTS

These pages provide more detail about the interesting facts found in the book. They are intended to be used by adults as a learning support to help young readers round out their knowledge of each sport featured in the *Let's Play* series.

**Pages 4–5**

**What Is Golf?** Golf is a sport in which a player uses a variety of clubs to hit a small ball into a hole. There are typically 18 holes on a golf course. The holes are played in order from first to last during a game of golf. Each hole features different designs, obstacles, and terrain. Golfers start each hole by hitting the ball, or teeing off, from the designated tee box for that hole. There are often several tee boxes, with adults typically teeing off farther from the hole than children do.

**Pages 6–7**

**What I Wear** Most golf courses have strict dress codes. People must wear the proper clothing in order to play. Golfers wear pants or shorts and a collared shirt. The shirt must be tucked into the pants. Pants must be semi-formal, such as khakis. Jeans and cargo pants are not allowed. Shorts follow similar rules to pants. Jogging or swimming shorts are not allowed. Shirts can be long sleeved, short sleeved, button-up, or pull-over. Golfers also wear special golf shoes.

**Pages 8–9**

**What I Need** Golfers use a wide variety of clubs. The tee-off shot is usually taken with a large, heavy club called a wood. Most other shots are taken with smaller clubs called irons. Special clubs, such as a sand wedge, help golfers play the ball in specific situations, including sand traps. The putter is a flat club used to push the ball along the ground. Woods and irons are numbered. The number refers to the angle of the club's striking surface, or head. Higher numbered clubs lob the ball higher into the air, while lower numbered clubs shoot the ball lower and farther.

**Pages 10–11**

**Where I Play** Golf courses have either 9 or 18 holes spread out over a huge outdoor area. Most courses feature trees, ponds, and rolling hills. Golfers navigate through the course, hitting their balls around water hazards, sand traps, and trees to reach each hole. Some holes might be as short as 100 yards (90 meters), while others may be more than 600 yards (550 m). Each hole features a tee box, a strip of moderate-length grass called a fairway, a border of tall grass called a rough, and a green. The green is an area of short grass around the hole.

**Warming Up** Golf is not as physically demanding as some other sports. However, it is still important to do a proper warm up before playing golf. Warming up loosens muscles and reduces the chance of injury. Before golfing, it is important to stretch all of the major muscle groups, including the arms, shoulders, back, and legs. A warm up should include both stretching and light activity. When warming up, it is best to start easy and gradually build up the intensity toward the end.

**Playing the Game** Each hole on a course has a par. This is how many strokes, or shots, it should take to finish the hole. Golfers try to finish each hole either on or under par. Finishing one under par is called a birdie, and two under par is called an eagle. Golfers try to avoid finishing above par. One above par is called a bogey, and two above par is a double bogey. Golfers keep track of their score on each hole. They write their score on a score card.

**Winning the Game** In golf, the lowest score wins. Golfers add their scores from each hole, and the player with the lowest score wins. Golfers often keep track of their score in terms of par. For example, when playing on a par 70 golf course, a golfer who finishes with a score of 65 is said to have finished five strokes under par. A golfer finishing with a score of 72 would be two strokes over par. In this case, the first golfer wins the match by seven strokes.

**Team Play** Golf is sometimes played as a team sport. Usually, two people will form a team and play against another two-person team. Teams may be all male, all female, or mixed, with a man and a woman making up the team. Teams can either play as a foursome or as a fourball. In foursome play, each team has one ball, and both players take turns hitting it. In fourball, each player uses his or her own ball. Only the lowest score on each hole counts toward the team's total.

**I Love Golf** Playing golf helps people stay active and healthy. Golf relies more on skills than physical ability, but it still provides a good form of exercise. Playing golf promotes physical fitness and hand-to-eye coordination. In order to get the most benefit from playing golf, it is also important to eat healthful foods. These foods—such as fruits, vegetables, and grains—give the body the energy it needs to perform its best.

# KEY WORDS

Research has shown that as much as 65 percent of all written material published in English is made up of 300 words. These 300 words cannot be taught using pictures or learned by sounding them out. They must be recognized by sight. This book contains 47 common sight words to help young readers improve their reading fluency and comprehension. This book also teaches young readers several important content words. These words are paired with pictures to aid in learning and improve understanding.

| Page | Sight Words First Appearance |
|------|------------------------------|
| 4 | am, I, play, to |
| 5 | closer, off, than, the, time |
| 6 | a, and, get, with |
| 7 | have, most, up |
| 8 | different, each, is, many, my, of |
| 9 | air, in |
| 10 | for, go, has, me |
| 11 | on, some |
| 12 | before |
| 13 | day, every, like |
| 14 | at, first, our, we |
| 15 | take, their |
| 16 | into, try |
| 18 | on, other, sometimes, two |
| 19 | same |

| Page | Content Words First Appearance |
|------|--------------------------------|
| 4 | golf, today |
| 5 | adults, hole, kids |
| 6 | collar, pants, shirt |
| 7 | courses, dress code |
| 8 | clubs |
| 9 | ball |
| 11 | driving range |
| 13 | pro golfers |
| 14 | friends, shots, tee |
| 17 | score, win |
| 18 | players, team |
| 19 | fact, teammates |